NATIONAL GEOGRAPHIC

# The Yard Sale

Gare Thompson

# Contents

# Having a Yard Sale

Jason wants a skateboard. His friend Carla would like to buy a new CD. How can they get the money to buy these things?

Jason has a lot of old toys and books. Carla has old toys, too. They both have clothes that do not fit. They will sell these things. They will have a yard sale. They will make money by selling things they no longer want or need.

# Planning the Yard Sale

**Carla and Jason have a lot of work to do.**

**They make a list.**

## Things to Do

1. Pick where and when to have the sale.
2. Make posters to tell people about the yard sale and hang them up.
3. Collect items to sell.
4. Price the things for sale.
5. Make cookies to sell at the yard sale.
6. Set up the table with the things for sale.

Jason's dad says they can have the sale in their yard. The sale will be next Saturday.

Carla and Jason make posters. They hang up the posters. They tell their friends about the sale. They hope many people will come.

Carla and Jason decide what to charge for their things. Some things will cost more than others.

Books will cost 50¢.

Toys will sell for $2.00.

Video games will sell for $5.00.

Carla and Jason will sell cookies, too. Carla's mom will help them make the cookies. Cookies will cost 25¢.

It is Saturday morning. Carla and Jason set out the things they are going to sell. Soon, friends and neighbors will come.

# Working at the Yard Sale

Carla and Jason have their first customer.
A friend wants to buy Jason's old train set.
It used to be one of Jason's favorite toys,
but he doesn't play with it any more.
Jason sells the train set.

A neighbor buys three pairs of shorts for her little girl. The three pairs of shorts cost $3.00. She gives Jason a five dollar bill. This is more money than the shorts cost. Jason gives his neighbor change. He gives her $2.00.

Carla's friend wants to buy five books, but he doesn't have enough money. He asks if she'll sell him five books for the price of four.

Carla agrees to sell five books for the price of four. She wants to sell as many books as she can.

The sale is almost over. To sell as many things as possible, Carla and Jason lower their prices. Carla makes a new sign that says, "Everything must go. Make us an offer."

A friend asks Jason if he'll sell the rest of the video games for $1.00 each. He agrees.

The sale is over. Almost everything has been sold. Carla and Jason eat the rest of the cookies. They pack up the toys and books that are left. They will give them away. They will give them to a group that helps families in need.

# Sharing Their Earnings

Carla and Jason count the money they earned. They made a total of $52.00. They split the money evenly. Each one gets $26.00.

Jason did not make enough to buy the skateboard he wants. He will save his share of the money.

Next month his grandmother will send him money for his birthday. He'll add his birthday money to the money he made at the yard sale. Then he should have enough money for the skateboard.

Carla buys the new CD she wanted. The CD cost less than the money she made, so she has money left to save, too.

Carla brings the CD over to Jason's house so he can listen to it. Carla and Jason both like the CD. They decide she's made a good purchase.

Carla and Jason agree they had a good yard sale. It was hard work, but it was fun, too. They made money by selling things they no longer wanted or needed.

Friends and neighbors got things they wanted at a good price. Everyone went home happy.